THE STORY OF
JOAN OF ARC

MAURICE BOUTET DE MONVEL

WITH AN INTRODUCTION BY
GERALD GOTTLIEB

DOVER PUBLICATIONS, INC.
MINEOLA, NEW YORK

Planet Friendly Publishing
✓ Made in the United States
✓ Printed on Recycled Paper
  Text: 10%   Cover: 10%
Learn more: www.greenedition.org

GREEN
EDITION

At Dover Publications we're committed to producing books in an earth-friendly manner and to helping our customers make greener choices.

Manufacturing books in the United States ensures compliance with strict environmental laws and eliminates the need for international freight shipping, a major contributor to global air pollution.

And printing on recycled paper helps minimize our consumption of trees, water and fossil fuels. The text of *The Story of Joan of Arc* was printed on paper made with 10% post-consumer waste, and the cover was printed on paper made with 10% post-consumer waste. According to Environmental Defense's Paper Calculator, by using this innovative paper instead of conventional papers, we achieved the following environmental benefits:

Trees Saved: 8 • Air Emissions Eliminated: 687 pounds
Water Saved: 3,307 gallons • Solid Waste Eliminated: 201 pounds

For more information on our environmental practices, please visit us online at www.doverpublications.com/green

Bibliographical Note

The Story of Joan of Arc, first published by Dover Publications, Inc., in 2010, is an unabridged republication of the work originally published as *Joan of Arc* by The Century Company, New York, in 1912. An Introduction by Gerald Gottlieb is included in this edition.

Library of Congress Cataloging-in-Publication Data

Boutet de Monvel, Louis-Maurice, 1851–1913.
    [Jeanne d'Arc. English]
    The story of Joan of Arc / Maurice Boutet de Monvel.
        p. cm.
    Includes bibliographical references.
    ISBN-13: 978-0-486-47026-9
    ISBN-10: 0-486-47026-1
    1. Joan, of Arc, Saint, 1412–1431—Juvenile literature. 2. Christian women saints—France—Biography—Juvenile literature. 3. France—History—Charles VII, 1422–1461—Juvenile literature. I. Title.

DC103.5.B6813 2010
944'.026092—dc22
[B]
                                                                                2009033836

Manufactured in the United States by Courier Corporation
47026101
www.doverpublications.com

Preface by the Author

On the 22nd of October, 1422, Charles VI. died, leaving his kingdom with the hand of his daughter, by the treaty of Troyes, to Henry V., King of England.

War had devastated our country for more than a century, but our independence had never been so menaced before.

Masters of Guyenne, allied on one side to the Duke of Burgundy, supported on the other by the Duke of Brittany, the English held the north and the centre of France as far as the Loire. Orléans, then besieged, opposed one last obstacle to their southward march ; but the helpless city was on the point of yielding.

The Dauphin, Charles VII., had taken refuge at Bourges ; a sorry King, without an army, without money, without energy. A few courtiers still disputed among themselves the last favours of the sinking monarchy, but none of them had the ability to defend it. Across a country stricken by famine, the remains of the royal army—bands of vagabonds from all quarters, reduced and demoralized by their recent defeats at Cravant and at Verneuil—were retreating, incapable of further effort.

Everything was lacking—men, means, even the will to resist. Charles VII., despairing of his cause, meditated flying to Dauphiné, perhaps even across the mountains to Castille, abandoning his kingdom, his rights, and his duties.

After the madness of Charles VI., the indolence of the Dauphin and the selfishness and incompetence of the nobility, had completed the ruin of the country, our very race was on the verge of losing its national existence.

At that moment, there rose up, in an obscure village on the borders of Lorraine, a little peasant girl. Moved with pity by the distress of the unhappy people of France, she had felt, deep in her heart, the first quiver of alarm in her motherland. With her weak hand she picked up the great sword of conquered France, and, making her tender breast a bulwark against so many miseries, she drew from the energy of her faith the force to raise the downcast spirits of her people, and to wrest our land from the victorious English.

"I come on behalf of our Lord God," she said, "to save the kingdom of France." And she added, "It is for this that I was born." The holy maid was indeed born for this; for this also, basely betrayed to her enemies, she died amidst the horrors of the most cruel torture, abandoned by the King whom she had crowned and by the people whom she had saved.

Open this book with reverence, my dear children, in honour of the humble peasant girl who is the Patroness of France, who is the Saint of her country as she was its Martyr. Her history will teach you that in order to conquer you must believe that you will conquer. Remember this in the day when your country shall have need of all your courage.

B. M.

April, 1896.

INTRODUCTION

It was a cruel and brutal time; and it was a sad time for France. The year was 1429. The Hundred Years' War was almost over. The endless battles and skirmishes in which the French fought the English or the Burgundians had devastated the lovely countryside of France. The land was ravaged by soldiers who marched back and forth across it on their murderous errands, burning fields and looting villages as they went. Roads were overgrown; brigands roamed the forests; travel between towns was very dangerous.

The kingdom of France was ruled by the Dauphin Charles, whose father, King Charles VI, had suffered bouts of madness before dying. There were those who said that the Dauphin's real father had been not King Charles VI but the king's brother, and therefore the Dauphin was not the legitimate heir to the throne. His mother the queen would neither deny nor confirm the rumor. The Dauphin consequently lived in great self-doubt and guilt, and he could not muster up the courage to have himself crowned.

And the war was going very badly for the French. All the country north of the Loire was controlled by the enemy—the English under John, Duke of Bedford, and their allies the Dukes of Burgundy. Paris itself was in the hands of the English. Orléans, the city that was the key to the Loire Valley and the gateway to the entire south, was under heavy siege. French armies had suffered a long string of defeats and were feeble and demoralized. Orléans seemed doomed. And when this last citadel fell, nothing would prevent the enemy from sweeping south beyond the Loire and overrunning all the rest of the French kingdom.

At this moment, the darkest in the history of France, a miracle took place. It began in Lorraine on the eastern frontier, in a small piece of territory controlled by Robert de Baudricourt, a captain loyal to the French ruler. A seventeen-year-old peasant girl—uneducated, but in the grip of a profound faith in God, and very insistent—had come to Baudricourt talking of visions and voices. She claimed that the figures of saints appeared before her, lit by a beautiful light, and that she heard their voices. They spoke to her often, and with great urgency, and they told her that she had been chosen to save France from its enemies. They bade her drive away the army besieging Orléans and take the Dauphin to Rheims, where he would be crowned King of France.

Robert de Baudricourt was, to say the least, skeptical. For a long time now, a prophecy had traveled about the countryside and through the villages; it said that one day a young girl would come to rescue France. And many a young woman had deluded herself that she could fulfill the prophecy. They all seemed mad, but this young girl, who was named Jeanne d'Arc—Joan of Arc—was different somehow. People took her seriously. Even some of the veteran soldiers under Baudricourt believed in her. To Baudricourt she said: "I am come before you from my Lord . . . my Lord wishes that the Dauphin be made king . . . and it is I who will take him to be crowned."

"Who is your Lord?" Baudricourt asked.

"The King of Heaven," Joan answered serenely.

And when he finally agreed to send her to the Dauphin, she said: "I was born to do this."

How do we know these things? Much of our information comes from eyewitnesses who testified at the two great trials of Joan of Arc, and whose words are preserved in the detailed, copious trial records. The first of these two proceedings was the Trial of Condemnation, in 1431, which led to Joan's execution for heresy; and the second was the Trial of Rehabilitation, which began in 1450. By then Joan had been dead for nineteen years, but many people, high and low, who had known her personally were still alive. The story that emerges from the trial records and from other contemporary chronicles and documents is not a long one. Joan the Maid, as she came to be known, was taken by Baudricourt's men to the French royal court. There she promptly recognized the Dauphin Charles, though he was disguised as one of his own courtiers. They spoke together in private, and she won his confidence immediately. What she said to him is not known, but it is likely she told the fearful, self-doubting monarch that she knew for certain he was the legitimate ruler of France, and that she had been sent by God to have him crowned. Joan was then tested by an ecclesiastical court, and she convinced the high churchmen that she was not a sorceress, that Saints Michael, Catherine, and Margaret *did* appear to her, and that she did indeed hear their voices and converse with them. And then she went on to her great triumphs, leading and inspiring French troops to victories, first at Orléans, where the enemy besiegers were driven off and the city liberated, and then at one fortress after another along the Loire Valley, culminating in a great rout of the enemy at Patay. Obeying her voices, she then achieved her dream of bringing the Dauphin to Rheims, where she saw him crowned King Charles VII of France. With her curious mixture of blind bravery and naïve gentleness (she loved the banner she carried in battle "forty times more than her sword"), Joan gave the French a new confidence and pride. She told them: "In God's name the soldiers will fight, and God will give the victory." She fanned a flame of patriotism in France that would burn forever. She became truly beloved of the multitude.

The nobles of the court, however, were less enthusiastic about the Maid; and Charles VII, his kingdom more secure now, had little further need of Joan. But the Maid still heard her voices, and she was still possessed by a burning urge to drive the enemy from the soil of France. She led troops in an attempt to take Paris from the English. The attempt failed. By now Joan had acquired a taste for fine clothing, and for masculine attire. She would dress in the elegant clothes of a nobleman of the court; she would go into battle wearing a splendid, flowing robe over her armor. Fighting in a skirmish at Compiègne, she suddenly found herself surrounded. A Burgundian soldier seized her robe and dragged her from her horse. She was taken prisoner. No one came forward to rescue or ransom her. The French king and his court watched and did nothing as the Burgundians sold her to the English. (The price was high—ten thousand livres.) The English announced that Joan the Maid would go on trial as a witch and a heretic.

The trial could have but one possible outcome. The English had bought her to burn her, and in the end nothing less would satisfy them. Joan of Arc died at the stake in the city of Rouen in May, 1431. Ten thousand people crowded into the square to watch. Some of the onlookers said later that when the executioners lit the fire a white dove flew up from the center of it. Others claimed that, outlined in the flames, they had seen the letters J E S U S. And the old chronicles tell of still other wondrous things, for as the flames rose above the pyre in Rouen, so rose up the legend of Joan the Maid, the savior of France. Upon that legend were nurtured French courage and hope, and a new feeling of unity. That, in the end, was the achievement of Joan of Arc.

S uch are the bare bones of the story. Joan of Arc was a visionary—devout, energetic, stubborn, ignorant but intelligent, gifted with military genius, and aflame with her mission. She became France's national heroine. In 1896 a fellow countryman of the Maid, an artist named Louis-Maurice Boutet de Monvel, set out to celebrate her achievements in a book for children. By then, of course, Joan had been revered in France for nearly five centuries. There had been countless illustrated versions of her story, for children of every age. But Boutet de Monvel now managed to create a new masterpiece. His *Jeanne d'Arc* would be more admired and loved, and would influence more artists and illustrators, than any other children's book of its era.

Boutet de Monvel was born in 1851 in Orléans, a city that had been obsessed with Joan of Arc ever since the Maid delivered it from siege in 1429. As a boy in Orléans he saw the name of the young heroine everywhere—on streets and squares, on public statues, on boxes of candy. The boy became an art student, and by 1874, at the age of twenty-four, he was an academic painter, exhibiting at the Paris annual Salon. Early in his career he turned to the illustration of magazines and books for children, and here he enjoyed success both financial and artistic. (At the same time he pursued another career, with even happier financial results, becoming international society's painter of choice for portraits of children.) Among the children's books he illustrated in the 1880s was *La Civilité puérile et honnête,* a work on etiquette for the young in the manner of the French courtesy books, which had a history going back to the Middle Ages (though Boutet de Monvel's treatment was somewhat tongue-in-cheek) . He also illustrated a selection of La Fontaine's *Fables.* In both works he demonstrated an ability to reconsider and reinvigorate a time-worn theme, to take a traditional subject and make something new of it.

This ability came into play again in 1896, when he took as a subject the figure that had been omnipresent in his Orléans childhood—Joan of Arc. Inspiration, he later wrote, came to him in Paris, as he stood in the Place des Pyramides before the gilded statue of the Maid, stiff and erect on her charger, brandishing her sword toward the Tuileries. The theme, even the inspiration, were hardly new. But Boutet de Monvel, with his special talent for quickening the traditional, produced a series of pictures that would be his *chef-d'oeuvre*, his own monument to the Maid.

For this new children's book he not only painted the pictures but also wrote the text. And a comment is perhaps necessary here about that text. Boutet de Monvel, it must be remembered, was a painter, not a writer. Even less was he a scholar; and consequently some of the facts in the book have been called into question. But it must also be remembered that Boutet de Monvel's *Jeanne d'Arc* was a work of its time. It should be judged as such. Consider the book's title page, upon which the Maid, in mediaeval armor, leads eager French riflemen dressed in the uniforms of 1896. Presumably she is leading them to a victory, one that perhaps will help the nation forget the defeat suffered by French arms in the Franco-Prussian War of 1870–71. The battles listed on the standard the riflemen bear are those of Napoleon's pre-Waterloo triumphs. Boutet de Monvel is calling for, or dreaming of, a resurgence of the military glories won by not only Joan the Maid but also the Emperor Napoleon. Nor is this title-page propaganda absent from the pages that follow, even though they are set in the Middle Ages. Boutet de Monvel's pictures may depict the fifteenth century, but his writing is infused with the nationalistic fervor of the 1890s. One can hardly expect to find in it the balance, the measured reason of an ideal historian.

So much for Boutet de Monvel the writer. Boutet de Monvel the artist is quite another matter. The text of *Jeanne d'Arc* may be flawed, but pictorially the book is a work of genius. It was recognized as such from the very first. "Unique," one critic called it. Indeed it was; but its images were rooted in the past. Although the flat, shadowless coloring of the pictures was reminiscent of Japanese prints (which had been much in vogue in France, witness Gauguin), or of children's paintings, many of the images had a more distant source. It was certainly a more logical source, for it was contemporaneous with the Maid herself. We know that Boutet de Monvel read mediaeval chronicles—Froissart, no doubt, and Monstrelet—from which he surely took the events, the dramatic confrontations, of his *Jeanne d'Arc*. But did he not perhaps also pore over the illuminations in mediaeval manuscripts? The massed groupings of men and horses, the stylized backgrounds, and above all the opulent detail of robe and wall hanging, are all to be seen in illuminated manuscripts from early fifteenth-century France, the time and place of the Maid's life. They can be seen, for example, on the vellum leaves of the *Très Riches Heures du Duc de Berry,* illuminated by the Limbourg brothers, and in work that the Boucicaut Master produced for Charles VI, the father of Joan's feckless and ungrateful Dauphin.

However one may speculate about the pictorial sources of Boutet de Monvel's greatest creation, its influence was pervasive on the children's books that followed. That is why its pictures seem so familiarly modern to us today, nearly a century after the artist produced them to transport and inspire children and to do homage to the peerless heroine of his own childhood.

Boutet de Monvel's *Jeanne d'Arc* was originally published in 1896, in Paris. A copy of that first edition is among the rare early children's books in the collections of The Pierpont Morgan Library in New York. The present edition, prepared from the Morgan copy, is the first edition since the nineteenth century which faithfully reproduces Boutet de Monvel's extraordinary colors and compositions. It thus enables a new generation of children and adults to experience this important classic of book illustration in all the freshness and subtlety of its original colors and all the drama of its brilliant, moving scenes.
The French text written by Boutet de Monvel was first translated into English in 1897, by A. I. du Pont Coleman.

Gerald Gottlieb
Curator of Early Children's Books
The Pierpont Morgan Library
New York City

THE STORY OF

JOAN OF ARC

Joan was born on the 16th of January, 1412, at Domremy, a little village of Lorraine, dependent on the bailiwick of Chaumont, which was held from the Crown of France. Her father's name was Jacques d'Arc, her mother's Isabellette Romée ; they were honest people, simple labouring folk who lived by their toil.

Joan was brought up with her brothers and sister in a little house which is still to be seen at Domremy, so close to the church that its garden touches the graveyard.

The child grew up there, under the eye of God.

She was a sweet, simple, upright girl. Everyone loved her, for all knew her kind heart, and that she was the best girl in the village. A brave worker, she aided her family in their labours ; by day leading the beasts to pasture or sharing the rough tasks of her father ; in the evening spinning at her mother's side and helping her in the house-keeping.

She loved God, and often prayed to Him.

One summer day, when she was thirteen years old, she heard a voice at midday in her father's garden. A great light shone upon her, and the archangel St. Michael appeared to her. He told her to be a good girl and to go to church. Then, telling her of the great mercy which was in store for the Kingdom of France, he announced to her that she should go to the help of the Dauphin and bring him to be crowned at Rheims. "I am only a poor girl," she said. "God will help thee," answered the archangel. And the child, overcome, was left weeping.

From this day, Joan's piety became still more ardent. The child loved to go apart from her playmates to meditate, and heavenly voices spoke to her, telling her of her mission. These, she said, were the voices of her Saints. Often the voices were accompanied by visions. St. Catherine and St. Margaret appeared to her. " I have seen them with my bodily eyes," she said later to her judges, " and when they left me I used to cry. I wanted them to take me with them."

The girl grew, her mind elevated by her visions, and her inmost heart keeping the secret of her heavenly intercourse. No one guessed what was going on in her—not even the priest who heard her confessions.

At the beginning of the year 1428, when Joan was sixteen, the voices became more urgent. The peril was great, they said, and she must go to help the King and save the kingdom.

Her Saints commanded her to seek out the Sire de Baudricourt, Lord of Vaucouleurs, and to ask of him an escort to conduct her to the Dauphin.

Not daring to tell her parents of her project, Joan went to Burey, to her uncle Laxart, and begged him to take her to Vaucouleurs. Her fervent prayers overcame the timidity of the cautious peasant, and he promised to go with her.

Baudricourt's reception of her was brutal. Joan told him how she was sent by God, to the end that he might send word to the Dauphin to stand firm, for God would send him help before the middle of Lent. She added that it was the will of God that the Dauphin should become King; that he should be crowned in spite of his enemies, and that she herself would lead him to his coronation. "The girl is crazy," said Baudricourt. "Box her ears and take her back to her father."

Joan returned to Domremy. But, urged again by her voices, she came again to Vaucouleurs, and saw the Sire de Baudricourt once more, with no better welcome.

Soon nothing was talked of at Vaucouleurs but the young
girl who went about saying openly that she would save the
kingdom, that some one must take her to the Dauphin, that God
willed it. "I will go," she said, "if I have to wear my legs
down to the knees."

The simple-hearted people, moved by her faith, believed in
her. A squire, Jean de Metz, influenced by the confidence of
the populace, offered to take her to Chinon, where Charles VII.
was. The poor folks, adding their mites together, raised the
money to clothe and arm the little peasant girl. They bought
her a horse, and on the appointed day she set out with a small
escort. "Go, and take the consequences!" Baudricourt threw
after her. "God keep you!" cried the multitude; and the women
wept as they saw her go.

The English and Burgundian party held the intervening country, and the little troop was obliged to pass over bridges occupied by the enemy. They had to travel by night, and hide through the day. Joan's companions, alarmed, spoke of returning to Vaucouleurs.

"Fear nothing," said she. "God is leading me, and my brothers from Paradise tell me what I ought to do."

So, on the twelfth day, Joan arrived at Chinon with her companions. From the hamlet of St. Catherine she had addressed a letter to the King, announcing her coming.

The court of Charles VII. was far from being of one mind as to the reception that ought to be given her. La Trémouille, the favourite of the moment, jealously guarding the ascendency he had acquired over the indolent spirit of his master, had decided to keep away any influence which might stir him out of his torpor. For two days the council debated whether the King should receive the inspired girl.

At that moment, news came from Orléans so disquieting that the partisans of Joan carried their point that the last chance of saving it should not be neglected. One evening, by the light of fifty torches, Joan was brought into the great hall of the castle, crowded with all the nobles of the Court. She had never seen the King.

Charles VII., not to attract her attention, wore a costume less splendid than that of his courtiers. At the first glance she singled him out, and knelt before him. "God give you a happy life, gentle Dauphin!" she said, "I am not the King," he answered; "yonder is the King." And he pointed out one of his nobles.

"You are he, gentle prince, and no other. The King of Heaven sends word to you by me that you shall be anointed and crowned." And, coming to the object of her mission, she told him that she was sent by God to aid and succour him; she demanded some troops, promising to raise the siege of Orléans, and to bring him to Rheims.

The King hesitated. The girl might be a sorceress. He sent her to Poitiers, to have her examined by learned men and ecclesiastics.

For three weeks they tormented her with insidious questions. "There is more in God's book than in yours: I do not know my A B C, but I come from the King of Heaven." When they objected that God had no need of men-at-arms to deliver France, she drew herself up quickly: "The soldiers will fight, but God will give the victory." There, as at Vaucouleurs, the people declared in her favour. They held her to be holy and inspired. The learned and powerful were forced to yield to the enthusiasm of the multitude.

The troops gathered at Blois. Joan arrived there, followed by the Duke of Alençon, the Marshal de Boussac, the Sire de Rais, La Hire and Xaintrailles.

On her banner she had embroidered the image of God and the names *Jesus, Mary*. She counselled her soldiers to put their consciences in order, and to confess their sins before going into battle. On Thursday, the 28th of April, the little army moved. Joan led the march, her banner flying, to the strains of the hymn "Come Holy Ghost." She wished to march straight to Orléans, but the leaders thought it more prudent to go by the left bank of the Loire.

The army and its convoy arrived at Chécy, two leagues above Orléans. When it came to passing the Loire, there were not enough boats. They transported Joan to the other bank with a part of her escort and the provision-train. The rest of the troops had to go back to Blois, and return to Orléans by the Beauce.

Joan said to Dunois, who came to meet her, "I bring you the best of help, that of the King of Heaven. It comes not from me, but from God himself, who, at the prayers of St. Louis and of Charlemagne, has had pity on the town of Orléans."

At eight in the evening, Joan entered Orléans. The people crowded to meet her. She passed by torchlight through the city, in the midst of a throng so dense that she could scarcely force her way. Men, women and children wished to get near her and at least to touch her horse, showing "as great joy as if they had seen God descend among them." They felt strengthened, says the journal of the siege, and as if relieved from attack by the divine power of the simple maid. Joan spoke kindly to them, promising to deliver them.

She asked to be taken to a church, wishing before all things to give thanks to God.

When an old man said to her, speaking of the English : "My daughter, they are strong and well-entrenched, and it will be a hard matter to get rid of them." She answered : "Nothing is impossible to the power of God."

And in fact her confidence infected everyone around her. The people of Orléans, so lately timid and discouraged, now excited by her presence to the pitch of fanaticism, wished to throw themselves on the enemy and to carry their works by assault. Dunois, fearing a check, decided to wait for reinforcements before beginning the attack. In the meantime, Joan summoned the English to depart and return to their own country, but they answered her with insults.

All the while no news came from Blois. Dunois, uneasy, went to hasten the coming of assistance, and he was just in time. The Archbishop of Rheims, Regnault de Chartres, the King's Chancellor, reversing the decision arrived at, was about to send the troops back to their quarters. Dunois obtained permission to lead them to Orléans.

On the morning of Wednesday, the 4th of May, surrounded by all the clergy of the city and followed by a great part of the population, Joan left Orléans. She advanced in a long procession through the English lines, heading the little army of Dunois, who passed, under the protection of the priests and of a girl, without the English venturing to attack them.

On the same day, Joan was resting, but woke up with a start. "Oh, my God!" she cried, "the blood of our men is flowing. That is not well done! Why did no one wake me? Quick, my arms, my horse!" Aided by the women of the house, she armed herself rapidly, leaped into the saddle, and galloped off, her standard in her and, making straight for the Burgundy gate.

14

The fact was that, without telling her, they had attacked the bastion of St. Loup. The attack had failed; the French were retreating in disorder. Joan rushed up, rallied them, and led them once more against the foe. In vain Talbot strove to support his comrades. For three hours the English resisted, but in spite of a desperate defence the bastion was taken.

Joan came back victorious into Orléans. But as, in the joy of her success, she was returning to the city across the field of battle, she felt her tender heart melt with pity at the sight of the dead and wounded, and she fell to weeping as she thought that they had died without confession. And she said that she had never seen French blood flow without her hair standing up on her head.

It was now a question how to follow up against the English this attack so happily begun.

The leaders, not over-pleased to let themselves be led by a peasant-girl, or to share with her the glory of success, met in secret to discuss the plan to be adopted.

Joan presented herself at the council; and, as the chancellor of the Duke of Orléans was trying to conceal the decisions which had been made, "Tell me what you have concluded and appointed," she cried, indignant at these subterfuges. "I am well able to keep a greater secret than that!" She went on: "You have been at your council, and I at mine; and, believe me, the counsel of God shall be accomplished and stand firm, while yours shall perish. Rise to-morrow very early, for I shall have much to do, more than I ever had before."

The next day, May 6th, she took the bastion of the Augustinians. On the 7th the attack on the Tournelles bastion was begun. Joan, descending into the moat, was raising a ladder against the parapet when an arrow from a cross-bow went through her, between the neck and the shoulder. She pulled out the iron; when someone offered to charm the wound she refused, saying that she would rather die than do anything contrary to the will of God. She made her confession, and prayed a long time while the troops were resting. Then, giving the order to begin the assault again, she threw herself into the thickest of the fight.

The bastion was captured, and all its defenders perished.

The following Sunday, the English were drawn up in order of battle on the right bank of the river. Joan forbade any attack to be made on them. When Mass had been celebrated, she said to those about her: "Look and see if the English have their faces towards us, or their backs." And as she heard that they were retiring in the direction of Meung, she said: "In the name of God, if they are going, let them go. It is not the pleasure of our Lord God that you should fight them to-day. You shall have them another time." So Orléans, besieged for eight months, was delivered in four days.

The news of the deliverance of Orléans spread far and wide, attesting in the sight of all the divinity of Joan's mission.

The holy maid, withdrawing from the gratitude of the people of Orléans, returned hastily to Chinon. She desired, profiting by the enthusiasm stirred up around her, to go at once to Rheims, taking the King with her to be crowned. He received her with great honours, but refused to follow her. He accepted the devotion of the heroic girl, but did not intend that her generous efforts should trouble the base indolence of his royal existence.

It was decided that Joan should go to attack the places still held by the English on the banks of the Loire.

On the 11th of June, the French occupied the suburbs of Jargeau. The next day at dawn, Joan gave the signal for battle. The Duke of Alençon wished to delay the assault. " On, gentle Duke," she cried, " to the attack ! Doubt not, this is the hour of God's pleasure. Work, and He will work with you ! " She herself mounted the scaling-ladder ; she was thrown down by a stone which struck her on the head. But she rose crying to her men " Up, up, friends ! The English are ours already ! " The ramparts were scaled, and the English, pursued as far as the town bridge, were taken or killed. Suffolk was made prisoner. On the 15th, the French gained possession of the bridge of Meung ; on the 16th they laid siege to Beaugency : and on the 17th the town surrendered.

On the 18th of June, Joan met near Patay the English
army under Talbot and Falstaff.

"We must fight them, in God's name," she said. "If they
were hung to the clouds, we should have them, because God
sends us to chastise them. Our noble King shall to-day have the
greatest victory yet!" She wished to join the vanguard, but
they restrained her. La Hire was charged to attack the English
and keep them back, to give the French troops time to come up;
but his onset was so impetuous that everything gave way before
him. When Jeanne rode up with her men-at-arms, the English
were retiring in disorder. Their retreat became a flight, and
Talbot was captured.

"You did not think, this morning," said the Duke of Alençon
to him, "that this would happen." "It is the fortune of war,"
Talbot answered.

The English lost 4,000 killed and 200 captured. No mercy was shown except to those who could pay a ransom ; the rest were put to death without pity.

One of them was struck so brutally that Joan leaped from her horse to help him. She raised the poor man's head, brought a priest to him, and helped him in his dying. Her heart was as full of pity for the English wounded as for her own partisans.

For the rest, she constantly exposed herself to blows, and was often wounded, but would never use her sword ; her standard was her only weapon.

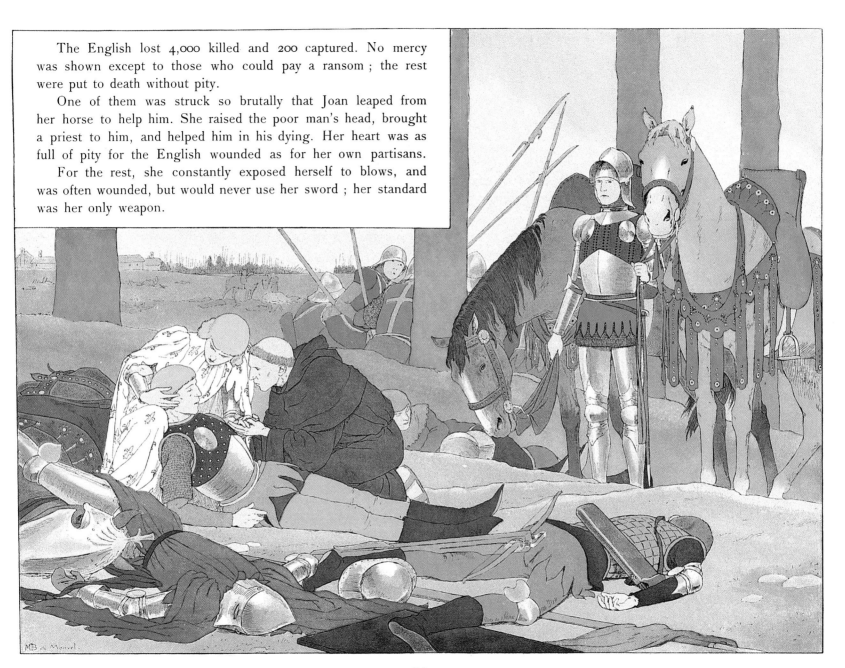

The English and Burgundian soldiers who formed the garrison at Troyes stipulated that they should be allowed to leave the town with all their possessions. Now these consisted principally of French prisoners. In drawing up the capitulation, nothing had been said about these unfortunates. But as the English left the town, dragging their captives with ropes round their necks, Joan threw herself across their path. " In God's name, " she cried, " you shall not take them away. " She forced them to deliver the prisoners to her, and the King to pay their ransom.

On the 16th of July, the King entered the town of Rheims at the head of his troops. The next day the ceremony of coronation took place in the Cathedral, before a great concourse of all ranks. Joan stood behind the King, with her standard in her hand. When Charles VII. had received the holy unction and

26

the crown from the Archbishop, Regnault de Chartres, Joan threw herself at his feet clasping his knees and weeping hot tears. " O gentle Sire, " she said, " now is accomplished the pleasure of God, who willed that I should bring you to your city of Rheims, to receive the holy anointing which shows that you are truly King, and that to you must belong the kingdom of France." " All those who saw her at that moment," says the old chronicle, "believed more than ever that it was a thing come from God." " Oh the good, loyal people ! " cried the holy maid, as she saw the enthusiasm of the crowd. " If I must die, I should be most happy to be buried here."

Nothing was so touching as the attachment of the common people to Joan. It was a contest among them to kiss her hands or her clothes, or only to touch her. They brought little children to her that she might bless them ; beads and images for her to sanctify by the touch of her hand. And the humble girl put away graciously these marks of adoration, rallying the poor folks sweetly on their blind belief in her power. But she asked at what time the children of the poor went to communion, so that she might communicate with them. Her pity was ready for all who suffered, but her special tenderness was for children and for the lowly. She felt herself their sister, knowing that she was born of one of them. Later on, when they reproach her with permitting this adoration of the multitude, she will answer simply, " Many people were glad to see me, and they kissed my hands when I could not help it ; but the poor folks came freely to me because I never did anything to hurt them."

After the coronation at Rheims, Joan wished to make a sudden descent on Paris and recapture the capital of the kingdom. The King's indecision gave the English time to prepare their defence. The assault was repulsed; Joan was wounded by a dart in the thigh. They had to drag her away from the foot of the ramparts to make her abandon the conflict. The next day the King was unwilling to renew to attack, though Joan answered for its success. They had dragged him from place to place long enough; he was impatient to resume his indolent life.

This retreat, compelled by the worthlessness of Charles VII., and by the jealousy of his courtiers, was a terrible blow to Joan's prestige. She was no longer invincible in the eyes of all. The holy maid seems to have understood this, for before quitting Paris she left as a votive offering on the altar of St. Denis her hitherto victorious arms. She prayed long. Perhaps she had at this moment the presentiment that her glorious mission was ended, and that sad trials were in store for her. None the less she submitted, and, with the bitterness of death in her soul, followed the King to Gien. The army was disbanded, the courtiers considering that there had been enough fighting. Moreover, their jealousy made them think it time to put a stop to Joan's successes.

But Joan could not resign herself to the inaction which they wished to impose upon her. Left without support at the siege of La Charité, she understood that she must henceforth look for no aid from Charles VII. At the end of March, 1430, without taking leave of the King, she went to Lagny to rejoin the French partisans who were skirmishing with the English.

Now during Easter-week, after she had heard Mass and received communion in the church of St. James at Compiègne, she withdrew and wept, leaning against a pillar of the church. She said to some of the townsfolk and children who surrounded her : " My children and dear friends, I tell you that they have sold and betrayed me, and that I shall soon be delivered up to death. I beg you to pray for me, for I shall have no more power to save the King or the Kingdom of France."

On May 23rd, at Crespy, she learned that the town of Compiègne was closely surrounded by the English and Burgundians.
She went thither with four hundred men, and entered the town on
the 24th at daybreak. Then, taking with her a part of the garrison,
she attacked the Burgundians. But the English came upon her,
and the French gave back. "Think of nothing but striking them!"
cried Joan. "Their defeat lies in your hands." But she was
carried away by her retreating men. When they came under the
walls of Compiègne, they found the drawbridge raised and the
portcullis let down. Joan, however, with her back against the
bank of the moat, still defended herself. A whole troop rushed

upon her, and cried to her to surrender. "I have sworn and given my faith to Another," answered the brave girl, "and I will keep my oath to Him." But her resistance was in vain. Held by her flowing garments, she was dragged from her horse and captured. From the walls of the town the Sire de Flavy, Governor of Compiègne, saw her taken, but did nothing to bring her aid.

Joan was taken to Margny, amid the joyful shouts of her foes. The English and Burgundians, even to the Duke of Burgundy himself, crowded to see the witch, and found themselves in the presence of a girl of eighteen. She was the prisoner of Jean de Luxembourg, a penniless gentleman, who only cared to make a good profit from his prize. The King of France made no offer to ransom her.

Joan was imprisoned in the castle of Beaurevoir. Knowing that the English wished to buy her from the Sire de Luxembourg, and also that the siege of Compiègne was advancing and that the town must yield, she let herself drop one night from the top of the keep, with the help of leather straps which broke. She fell to the foot of the wall, and lay for dead. She recovered, however, from her fall; a more cruel fate was reserved for her. At the end of November she was delivered to the English for a sum of ten thousand livres.

Shut up in the dungeon of the castle at Rouen, she was guarded day and night by soldiers, whose insults and even brutality she was forced to bear, her chains not allowing her to defend herself. Meanwhile a tribunal, devoted to the English party and presided over by Cauchon, Bishop of Beauvais, was preparing for her trial. To the insidious questions of her judges the unhappy and saintly maiden had nothing to oppose but the uprightness and simplicity of her heart. "I am sent by God," she said. "I have nothing more to do here. Send me back to God, from whom I came."

She still had one support, that of her Saints. They alone had not forsaken her. She received counsel continually from her heavenly voices; St. Margaret and St. Catherine appeared to her in the silence of the night, and comforted her with kind words. When Bishop Cauchon asked her what they said, she answered: "They woke me up; I clasped my hands and asked them to counsel me. They told me to ask our Lord." "And what more did they tell you?" "To answer you boldly." And as the Bishop plied her with questions: "I cannot tell you all. I fear more to say anything that might displease them than I do to answer you."

One day Stafford and Warwick came to see her, with Jean de Luxembourg. As the latter jestingly said that he came to propose her ransom if she would promise never to bear arms against the English, she answered: " In God's name, you are mocking me, for I know that the English will put me to death, hoping after I am gone to win the kingdom of France ; but if they were a hundred thousand more, they should not have the kingdom." The Earl of Stafford, enraged, threw himself upon her, and would have killed her had not the bystanders intervened.

MB de Monvel.

Joan, treated as a heretic, was deprived of the consolations of religion. The sacraments were denied her. Returning from her examination, and passing with her escort before the closed door of a chapel, she asked the monk at her side whether the body of Christ lay within, begging him to let her kneel for a moment and pray. He consented ; but Cauchon, hearing of it, threatened him with the direst punishment if such a thing occured again.

However, the trial went too slowly to please the English. "Judges, you are not earning your pay!" they cried to the members of the tribunal. "I came to the King of France," said Joan, "on the part of God, the Virgin Mary, the Saints, and the Church triumphant in Heaven. To that Church I submit myself, my works, all that I have done or shall do. You say that you are my judges; take good heed what you do, for truly I am sent by God, and you put yourselves in great peril." The saintly heroine was condemned as a relapsed heretic, apostate and idolater, to be burnt in the Market-Place of Rouen. "Bishop, I die through you!" she said to Cauchon.

On the 30th of May, Joan confessed and received communion. Then she was conducted to the place of execution. When she reached the foot of the scaffold, she knelt down and invoked God, the Virgin, and the Saints. Then, turning to the Bishop, the judges, and her enemies, she begged them devoutly to have Masses said for her soul. She mounted the pile, begged for a cross, and died with the name of Jesus on her lips. All were weeping, even the executioners and the judges. " We are lost! We have burned a saint, " cried the English, as they fled from the place.

43